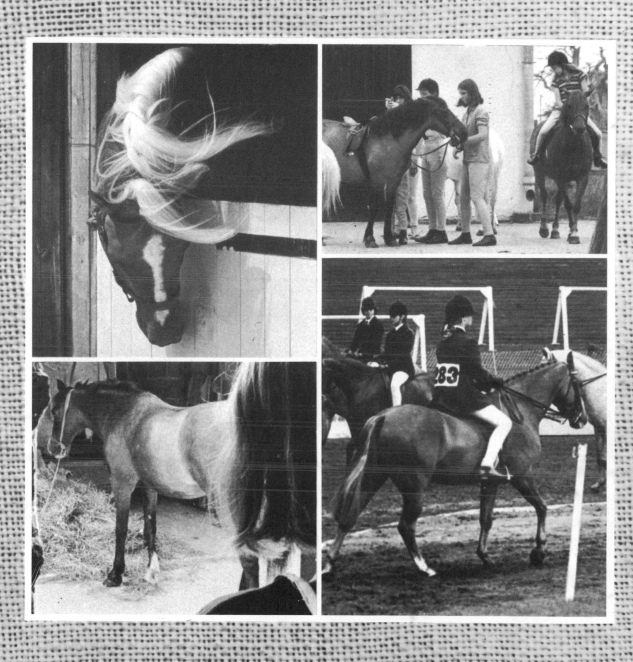

THE GOLDEN

Contents

© 1971 Thomas Nelson & Sons Limited
Reprinted 1974
Printed in Great Britain by
Hazell Watson & Viney Limited,
Aylesbury, Bucks
SBN 7238 0708 6

PONY BOOK

We all know what Ponies are; they're small horses.

We all know the tremendous appeal of Ponies; but what gives them this appeal? Why are they such entirely enchanting creatures?

There's more than one answer to that question . . .

First, Ponies have been part of our lives since before history began; don't forget that the "horses" people rode long ago are what we would now call ponies—the horse-sized mount was not always with us.

So we've known Ponies for a long, long time . . .

Second, they are small, and who among us can ever resist the appeal of the miniature.

NELSON YOUNG WORLD

THIS IS A PONY

A Pony, for a start, is a horse. . . .
All Ponies are Horses—
but only some Horses are Ponies. . . .
It's a matter of size.
Under fifteen hands—
That is a Pony.

This chap is a pony, even though he does
manage to look like a fine large steed.
He's only ten hands.

Shire and Shetland. Eighteen hands greets eight. But they're both splendid samples of their own sort.

Family Pony. Mum learned to ride on the Pony's Mum. . . .

Out to grass. She gets her bowl of oats each day, but grass is her main feed, which keeps her the way she's meant to be, just a friendly, easy-to-ride Pony. Too much oats, and she'd be too much of a handful for a novice rider.

GOLDEN PONY

Meet our cover-boy, the Golden Pony himself. He's a lively stallion named Ray, and he lives somewhere in Ireland, that green and splendid land of fine Horses.

. . . I rather enjoy looking out
from my home . . .

. . . to greet my friends . . .

. . . and to tell that pup what I think
of his yapping . . .

. . . and then of course I have my paddock . . .

. . . which is fine for a run . . .

10

. . . or I can eat it.

I'm a fine big pony,
and the world belongs to me!

11

Riding is the art of keeping a Pony between yourself and the ground . . .

OUT FOR A RIDE

A canter is a cure for every evil.

For more than a hundred centuries, when people needed to travel, they used horses— or rather ponies—for the big chaps were not all that numerous in ancient times, and mostly were for warriors. So ponies have been ridden by people since before history began. That's one good reason why it is such a natural thing to do, whether you dress up and do it in style, or you just take it easy in any old clothes. . . .

. . . . Today, people ride for the fun of it, and of course, the exercise.
A pause half way is something the ponies appreciate just as much as you do.

TALKING TO PONIES

*Whether horses understand what you say
is beside the point; there is no doubt
that they appreciate a kindly word.*

He's earned those rosettes for you,
so the polite and sensible thing is to thank him.

Say what you like, some ponies understand
every word you say. Just try thinking aloud,
on the lines of "You look as though you could
do with a bit more work, my lad," and see
that "I don't want to know" look come over
your pony.

Of course, there are those times when you've just got to say something.
It's all very well for a pony to be affectionate,
but this is ridiculous. . . .

19

RED INDIAN HORSE TALK

To start his horse the Blackfoot rider repeated the sound "sh" (made with the mouth open) several times. To slow down or stop the horse he called "ka" a number of times. Both commands were nonsense sounds, having no meaning except as horse commands. "Ka" was also the command given by men to keep their horses nearby and quiet after they dismounted in war or under other conditions when it was imperative for the horse to remain still. Women trained their best mares to stand still and submit to the bridle when their owners called "ka." Elderly men, who had stolen horses from the Cree, Crow, and Flathead in their youth, said those tribes did not use the same commands. They did not recall the commands used by those tribes, but remembered that horses stolen from them by Blackfoot warriors had to be taught to respond to Blackfoot verbal commands. Today all Blackfoot, whether or not they speak much English, employ the commands "whoa" and "giddap" to stop and start their horses.

ALL DRESSED UP

Bridles are business-like these days;
but it wasn't always so.
There was a time when a pony
could be proud of his trappings.

Have you ever thought that there's a very good reason why full-dress riding gear looks old fashioned? It's because it reflects the days when the horse was at his greatest— when there were no motor cars—and when people had had hundreds of years to work out the best sort of clothes for riding horses. That's why the elegant turn-out of horse and rider still counts a lot in the big horse shows. . . .

You'll never stop some people from showing off, though.

22

THE RIGHT TACK

Tack is what your mount wears; it isn't harness. Strictly, harness is for pulling carts and carriages . . .

Probably you're quite happy as long as you've got a bridle that your pony will "go" in. But just take a look at that tack on the right. No prizes offered, but can you sort out all those straps?

TACK . . . .

Horses sweat, tack gets tacky, and you've got to clean it.

Looks nice when it's clean, tack does.

But there's more to it than looking nice; Leave it dirty, and it gets stiff, hard, unbending; leave it dirty and it rots.

A stiff bridle is bad for the horse, and stiff reins are uncomfy for you.

And they break.

So . . . . Let not your tack get tacky.

Loose-boxes long bereft of life—
save mice, and things that crawl—
Shreds of old straw, half-way to dust,
and cobwebs over all;
Only sad ghosts of sounds and smells
now dwell in this old place,
only fond memories of dead days
of ride, and hunt, and race.
These bridles, stiffly hanging here,
full many a tale could tell,
of other young, high hopeful hearts,
who fell beneath a pony's spell.

DOING FOR PONIES

So who enjoys mucking out? But if a pony is going to be a pony, and not just another equine ungulate, then some things must be done for him that he cannot do himself.

Ponies are keen,
On being clean,
But are not able,
To cleanse a stable,
So it's their due
to look to you,
To take foul straw,
And bring them more,
To brush their backs,
To fill their lacks.
They thank you fully in return, you know,
With four hooves stepping out below. . . .

So sponge and brush,
And check for thrush,—
(Hooves should smell sweet,
should not make heat),
Watch for each worn and shaky shoe,
And get the Smith in to renew.

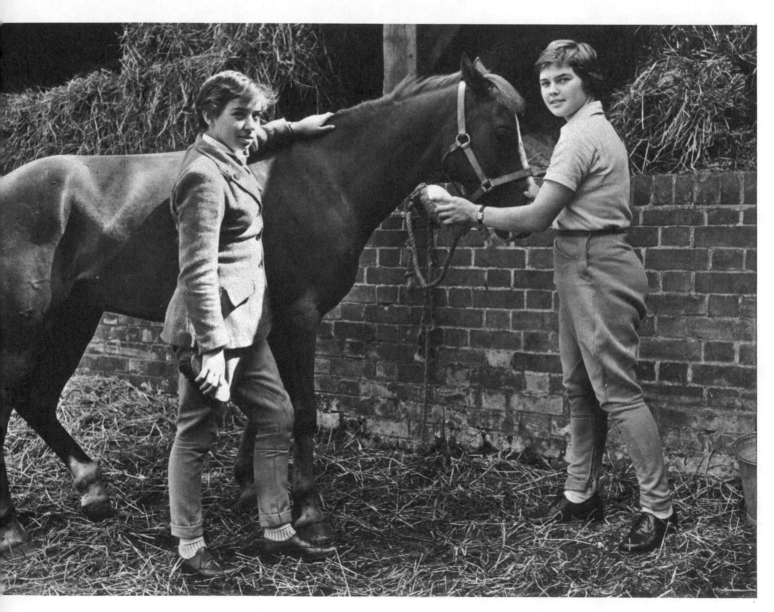

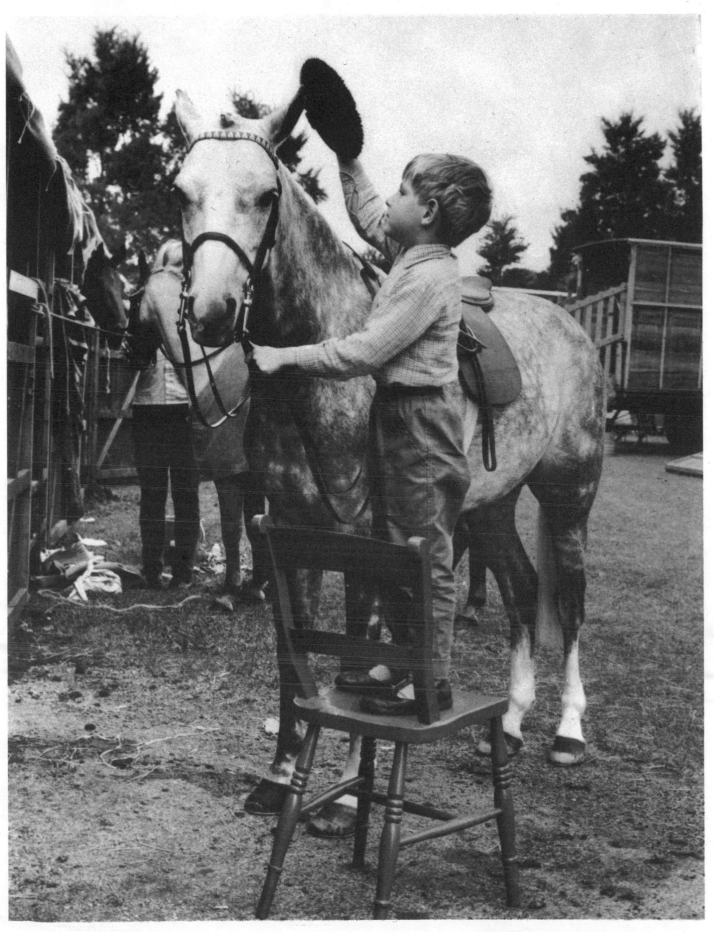

A pony kept in proper trim,
Is always sure you care for him,
And as we've said, your quid pro quo,
Is his four hooves at work below.

29

PONY TREKKING

Trekking, according to the Oxford Dictionary,
is making a journey by Ox-wagon.
But meanings change, and now trekking
is any sort of cross-country journeying.

You start at a farm, and with your guide, you all set out. Nobody really cares whether you've ever ridden a pony before, and the ponies are used to beginners. You pick it up as you go along.

At the end of the first day, you'll feel like a veteran . . . At the beginning of the second day, you'll feel like a board. The wise ones will tell you all sorts of things you should have done to avoid stiffness— but you soldier on, and the stiffness passes. If it's any consolation, it happens to everyone.

31

All in all, if there's wildness you'd be seeing, then it's pony trekking for you, for a pony will take you into the very midst of it, where the roads don't go. The guides— and the ponies—know the way, so you always end up with a good meal and a bed at the end of the day.

So you trek through the countryside, seeing
a whole splendid lot of it, for on the back
of a horse you're above the hedgerows, not
below 'em, as you are in a car.

And in the whole world, there's nowhere better
than that green land of horses, Ireland, for
Pony Trekking . . . And no better way to see Ireland.

WHAT PONIES THINK OF YOU...

One famous race-horse used to watch aeroplanes,
and clearly he must have thought about them.
Most ponies have a lot to do with people.
They must have thoughts about them . . .

"Pony shows they call them. Great fun . . . You can see
people doing all sorts of things. Beats me what they
see in watching ponies, though."

"Who's that coming?"
"It's old Jiggle-jiggle—and he's carrying a bridle."
"Let's go and stand in the middle of the pond!"

"She's a promising youngster.
Make a good rider, she will,
by the time I've done with her."

BUYING AND SELLING

"Look first at his feet." That advice to a buyer is more than two thousand years old, and still good. "For a handsome horse with bad feet is like a splendid house with poor foundations . . ."

TWICE AS MANY LEGS

Four legs go better far than two;
four legs below will carry you
over the hills and far away,
and back again, in a single day,
into green worlds so old and far,
you'd never reach them in a car.
Cars can't jump hedges, gates and streams—
Cars cannot reach this world of dreams . . .

A few words

from

a horse.

I have had a good deal to do with the subject-matter of this book, and I think that a lot of it is quite good. The author really seems to have tried to give us "a fair crack of the whip", as the saying is.

A lot of it seems pretty dull to me. So dull, in fact, that I wonder the author bothers to ride at all—let alone write about it. So if, after reading this, you read on: don't say that you haven't been warned.

There is a thing he has not said. I have never heard it mentioned, and I should like to record it on behalf of us all. It is to stress the peculiar mentality which develops from the fact that our senses are so far in front of our bodies and legs which they control (and, of course, twice the number of legs that a rider has got). Everything of any importance goes on behind us, as it were. This has a conditioning effect on the mind which amounts almost to apprehension; and one which must be very nearly incomprehensible to the average human who, by walking about on his hind legs, has managed to catch up with himself.

It's surprising how quick in the uptake some humans are,
if you just show them exactly how to trot.

There are times when having four legs
is a bit of a trial. . . .

WHERE PONIES DWELL...

The House is old,
   the hearth is cold,
The rooms are empty and
   the windows stare—
Long gone are they,
   far, far away
Who made their
   Homestead there.
Only this grey,
   recalls the day,
When here of life there
   was no lack—
And still she waits,
   watching the gates,
To see her people
   coming back.

Horses and Ponies are a privileged race.
When the fields are green, and the grass
is tender, their world is one huge dinner.

The grass is always greener on
the other side of the fence.

Green pastures—fine old trees for
shade—warm friendly stables.
These things and many more are the
marks of a homestead with horses
to it. That a house should have
its stables close by is a very
pleasant thing; it is also good
for the horses, who should see
their people coming and going at
all times as a normal part of their
lives. . . .

PONIES WITH WHEELS

*For untold centuries by far the best and quickest
way to move loads or passengers on dry land
was to use horses or ponies pulling carts or carriages . . .
It's only in the last century that the motor car has taken over.*

It's not so long ago that most people had their milk delivered by a pony. This chap is typical; cobby, patient, and intelligent enough to "learn the round". A good Milkman's pony got to know which houses to stop at nearly as well as the man he worked with.

"Not one horse in fifty that is good under saddle is equally so in harness, and vice versa." So wrote Sir George Stephen, in Queen Victoria's reign—but he'd have been wrong about this one. He was a champion show jumper in his day, and he never objected to obliging his family with two wheels behind him.

This is a trap—the seats run across the body, and you get in at the front. The two-wheelers that you board from the rear, and which have seats along each side, are called governess-carts.

As we've noted elsewhere, seeing and beholding is done best from the back of a horse. But if you are one of those who consider a horse to be "dangerous at both ends and uncomfortable in the middle", and you prefer four wheels beneath you to four legs, then you'll see a lot more of the countryside from a caravan than a car . . . Especially the Irish countryside.

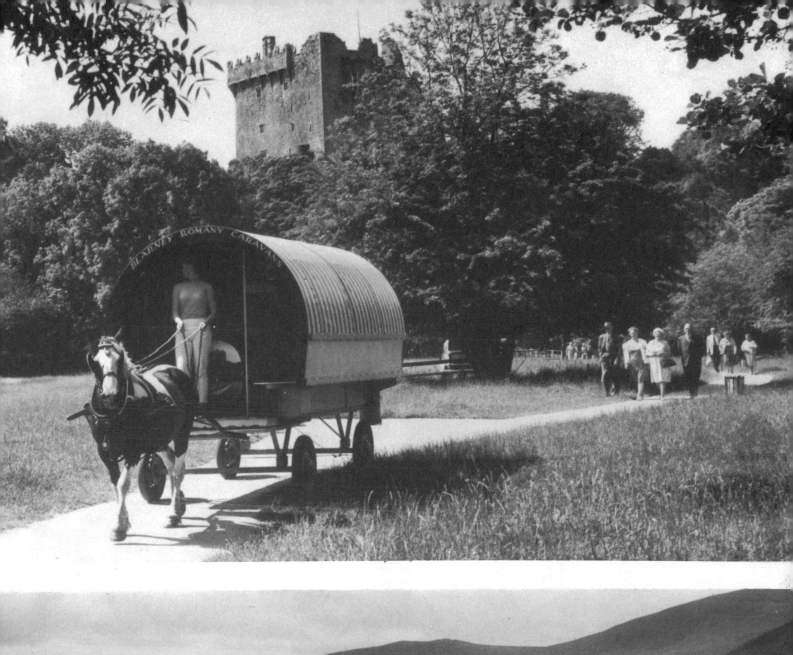

More than fifty years ago the last of the horse buses vanished from London's streets. Bus horses were of the same stamp as the artillery horses of those days. But read what an expert writer said of them, a century ago . . . "Heavy as a loaded omnibus looks, thoroughbreds would beat these artillery horses; but for work on London stones, where stopping and starting would fret the high bred horses, weight, strength, and short legs, carry the day."

SPEEDY WHEELS

Unless you were driving a chariot, you didn't encourage your harness horses to gallop . . .

A fine spanking trot was the best pace of a fine carriage horse. Today we only see the harness trotters in the show ring, where they are marked for style and turnout, rather than just for pace. In America, with featherweight two-wheeled "sulkies" behind them, trotters still race.

AMERICAN WORK PONY

There is one thing in the United States of America that has not changed since the eighteen fifties—the faithful cow-pony. There's a good and simple reason for this— the cow-pony does the job best. A good cow-pony can "cut out" and corner one single steer from a herd. Now you couldn't do that in a car—and you'd find it a tiring exercise on your own two feet. . . .

PADDLING AND POOTLING

Paddling is for fun—but Pootling, which is what the experts call mini-jumping, is a serious business. That pole won't knock off, you know . . .

Grey stone walls, and the sound
of horses. Built for horses, those
buildings were. Under that
steep-pitched roof is the hay loft.
You fork the hay off the wains
straight in through that red door
level with the guttering, and it's
there to be raked as it's needed
through the holes into the
hay-racks in the boxes below.
And it keeps the stables warm,
because the hay stops the heat
of them escaping through the
roof in cold weather.
A proper place for ponies, this.

ENTERTAINERS

Strange to say, the precise movements of the circus ring originated in the grim business of war. When men fought on horseback, exact obedience was a matter of life and death.

Star pony—a real show-biz trouper.
But these small ponies once worked hard
for their oats. For their size, they're
the strongest of all the horse breeds.
Once, they worked in the coal-mines . . .

Star rider. Paulina Schumann, posed
here with a friend in splendid Sicilian
cart-harness, is the rider of that
glamour pony two pages back.

Angel Peralta, on Mimosa. Their display
of skill is something to make you think;
Mimosa can even canter backwards!

HUNTING DAYS

Opinions may be mixed about the rights and
wrongs of hunting, but one thing is for
sure; it has produced some of the finest
all-round horses in the world. If a horse
or a pony is described as a 'Good Hunter'
in a sale catalogue, it is being given
the highest accolade of excellence
that horsemen recognise.

"Hunter" is not a breed. Any horse, or pony, can be a hunter—if he's good enough. Being a "Good Hunter" means having the strength and stamina to carry a rider for hours across almost any country, in any weather. It means being sound and sure-footed enough not to stumble, whatever the ground is like. It means being a very respectable jumper. It means having courage, combined with a good temper and a willing nature.
So what more could you ask of a horse?

Cats and Horses seem to go together;
There's many a kitten been born in
a manger . . .

FRIENDSHIPS

Friendships are strong among horses. These two are quite inseparable, and when, because of ways of men, the home they had known for so long was no more, the League for the Protection of Horses took them to Cherry Tree Farm to let them spend their remaining years— together.

"When you're as old as I am, son, you'll understand about things like trigonometry . . ."
"Oh, good—Can you eat it?"

FRIENDSHIPS

People who haven't even ridden a Pony
or a horse have read "Black Beauty",
and it is almost a catalogue of all
the friends and enemies a working horse
in the nineteenth century might have;
especially friends . . . .
Beauty belonged first to Squire Gordon,
the master of Birtwick Park, and one of
Beauty's companions of these early days
was "a fat little grey pony, with a thick
mane and tail, a very pretty head, and
a pert little nose."
This was Merrylegs . . . .

MR. BLOOMFIELD, the vicar, had a large family of boys and girls; sometimes they used to come and play with Miss Jessie and Flora. One of the girls was as old as Miss Jessie; two of the boys were older, and there were several little ones. When they came, there was plenty of work for Merrylegs, for nothing pleased them so much as getting on him by turns and riding him all about the orchard and home paddock, and this they would do by the hour.

One afternoon he had been out with them a long time, and when James brought him in and put on his halter, he said:

"There, you rogue, mind how you behave yourself, or we shall get into trouble."

"What have you been doing, Merrylegs?" I asked.

"Oh!" said he, tossing his little head, "I have only been giving those young people a lesson, they did not know when they had had enough, nor when I had had enough, so I just pitched them off backwards, that was the only thing they could understand."

"What?" said I. "You threw the children off? I thought you did know better than that! Did you throw Miss Jessie or Miss Flora?"

He looked very much offended, and said:

"Of course not, I would not do such a thing for the best oats that ever came into the stable; why, I am as careful of our young ladies as the master could be, and as for the little ones, it is I who teach them to ride. It is not them, it is the boys; boys," said he, shaking his mane, "are quite different; they must be broken in, as we were broken in when we were colts, and just be taught what's what. Boys, you see, think a horse or pony is like a steam engine or a thrashing machine,

IN THE ORCHARD

and can go on as long and as fast as they please; they never think that a pony can get tired, or have any feelings; so as the one who was whipping me could not understand, I just rose up on my hind legs and let him slip off behind—that was all; he mounted me again, and I did the same. Then the other boy got up, and as soon as he began to use his stick I laid him on the grass, and so on, till they were able to understand, that was all. They were not bad boys; they don't wish to be cruel. I like them very well; but you see I had to give them a lesson. When they brought me to James and told him, I think he was very angry to see such big sticks. He said they were only fit for drovers or gipsies, and not for young gentlemen."

"If I had been you," said Ginger, "I would have given those boys a good kick, and that would have given them a lesson."

WILD
PONIES

Sturdy Wild Ponies, from the moors, forests and waste-lands, are one of the great natural treasures of these islands. . . .

"Wild" ponies in the circus ring. As the
lights went up, these superb performers
acted the part of a wild herd, milling in
the morning mists . . . Then came the trainer
and their act climaxed in a precision display.

American wild ponies. These are all "strays"
from domesticated stock—for there were no
ponies or horses in America before the coming
of the white men.

New Forester. These are fine ponies, whose stock was improved in Victorian times by Arab stallions that were set free among them.

Born wild. Those neat little hooves have never touched a road; he'll get over his childhood ailments.

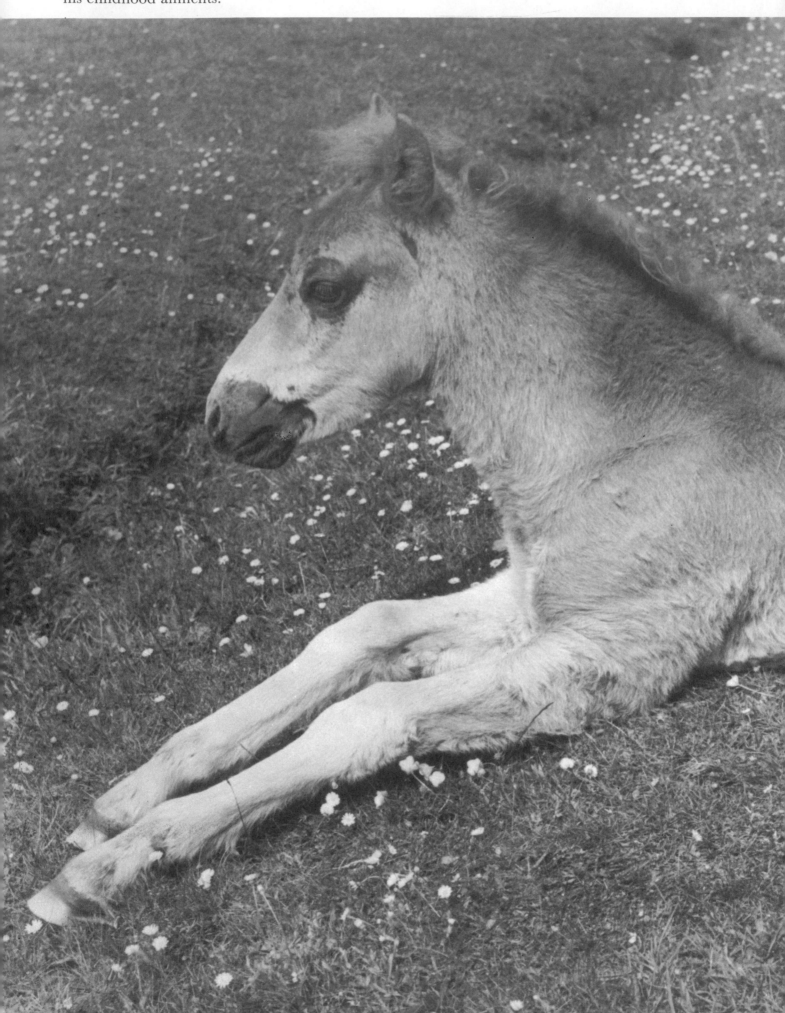

SOFTLY CATCHEE PONY

*You arrive in the paddock with a bridle
over one arm, and every pony in sight
knows exactly why you're there . . .*

Food is the answer; there's nothing quite like half an apple for catching a pony . . . or two ponies.

PONIES
MAKE
PICTURES

In the flat lands of the Ile de la Camargue in southern France are wide green pastures; it's horse country . . . .

. . . it's one of the best places in
the world to hunt ponies with a camera.

A classic "western" picture, this.
Fenced corral, and cow-ponies . . .

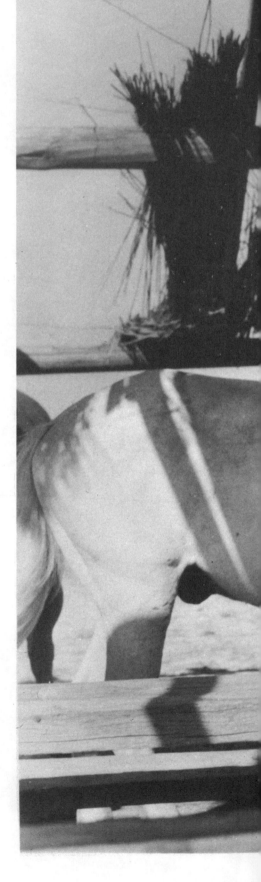

An open faced bridle with a curb-bit—
you may well think this is a "western"
too. Actually, it's the Camargue again.

PONIES
AT
SCHOOL

Lungeing is part of the education of a well-schooled Pony; by means of the long lungeing rein, he can be accustomed to the feel of a bit and bridle before he ever has a rider on his back. But even experienced Ponies, like this one, are worked on the long rein to keep them up to the mark.

Learning to ride is quite hard work . . .

. . . and it is a pleasant thing, for you and the pony, to sit down sociably for a rest once in a while.

THE YOUNG GENERATION

A new-born foal has been described as a collection of long legs tied together at the top with a very small body. . . .

The cannon (or shannon) bones
are as long as they will ever be
when the foal is born. They are the
long bones above the four hooves.
They will gain something in bulk,
but from end to end—joint to
joint—they stay the same right
through the horse's life.

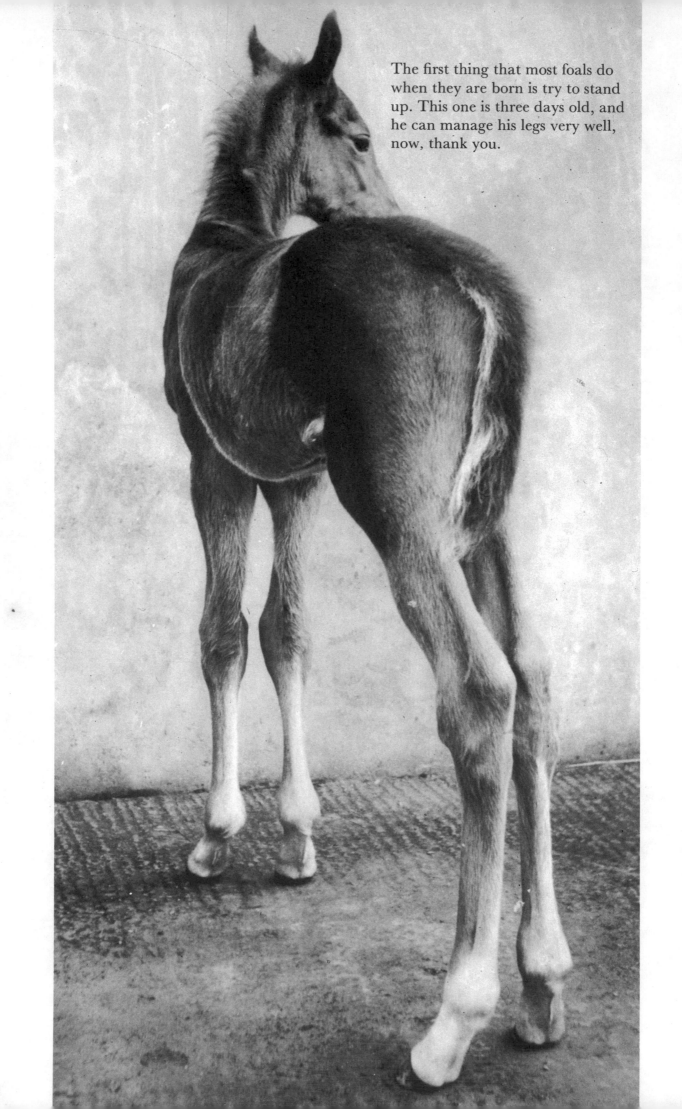

The first thing that most foals do when they are born is try to stand up. This one is three days old, and he can manage his legs very well, now, thank you.

OVER THE TOP

Throw your heart over first—
Your Pony will follow after it.

The First Leap.

Will you ever forget your first BIG competition?
There you stood, feeling terrible, trying to look as if you hadn't a care in the world, as far away from anyone who knew you as possible . . . . And then you saw all that daylight between Betty so-and-so and her saddle. And she was a veteran. . . . After that, you felt much better.

And here of Nature's kindly care
Behold a curious proof,
As nags are meant to leap, she puts
A frog in every hoof!

A big jump

is not

so much

a matter

of

how high

you fly,

but

how tightly

your pony

tucks up

his feet . . .

TAKING IT EASY

JUST PONIES

Ponies are horses which, in the course of history, learned to live in the wild moors and forests, on poo fodder. That's why they : small, and hardy.

TO SEE AND TO BEHOLD...

*Did you happen to notice, when you
first started riding, how much you
saw that you hadn't seen before?*

. . . . suddenly, from the saddle of a pony, the world is a much bigger place, filled with a wealth of things you just never noticed on your own two feet . . .

WORLD OF HORSES...

"Now," said the grandfather, "out with it. I'll not have you as companion to me this day, and you as silent as an image. What is it withdraws you from me entirely?"

The boy thrust out his underlip, kicked a stone at his feet, and replied: "It has nothing to do with you. You are not to blame. You were in Kenmare when it happened. I'm just thinking, planning you might say. I have made up my mind I don't like this world and the way it's run."

"So," said the man, "and you all of ten years. You're not the first to think the same, but usually there is more reason to enter the Street of the Misanthrope than you'd be having, I'd wager. What sort of a world would please you now? I'll see what I can do."

The boy turned and looked away to the edge of the next pasture where two yearling colts were nibbling each other's scraggy manes, registering laze and utter contentment. A strong blue light leaped into the eyes of the boy. "I'd like a world of horses. Nothing but horses, and you, of course. I can talk to horses. I know all their little ways."

"You do that, more than anyone I've ever known," replied the man.

Together these two, who so deeply understood each other, went down the hill to the paddock at Croghangeela under the tall trees.

HARD WORKING PONIES

*In the narrow galleries of coal-mines,
far below ground, many ponies once
toiled for their living . . .*

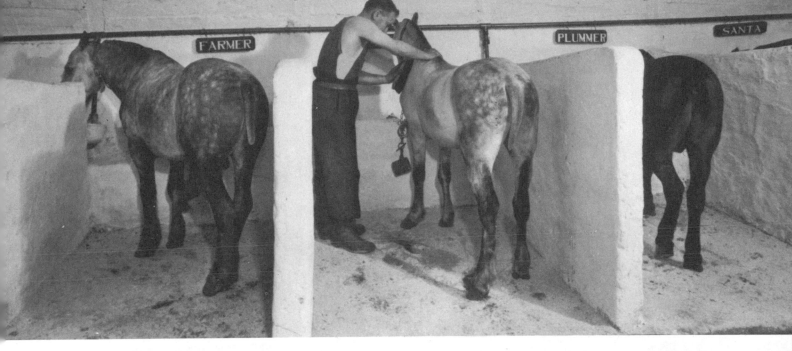

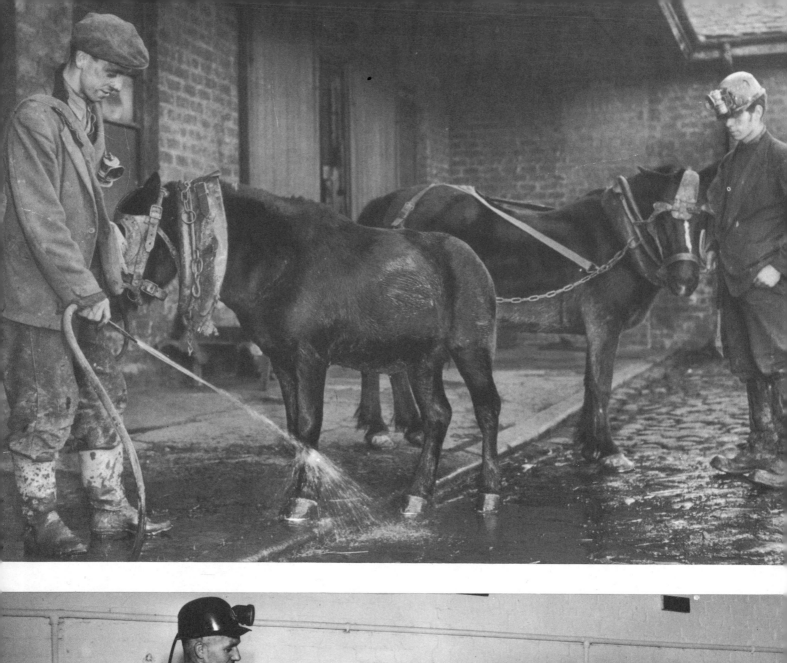
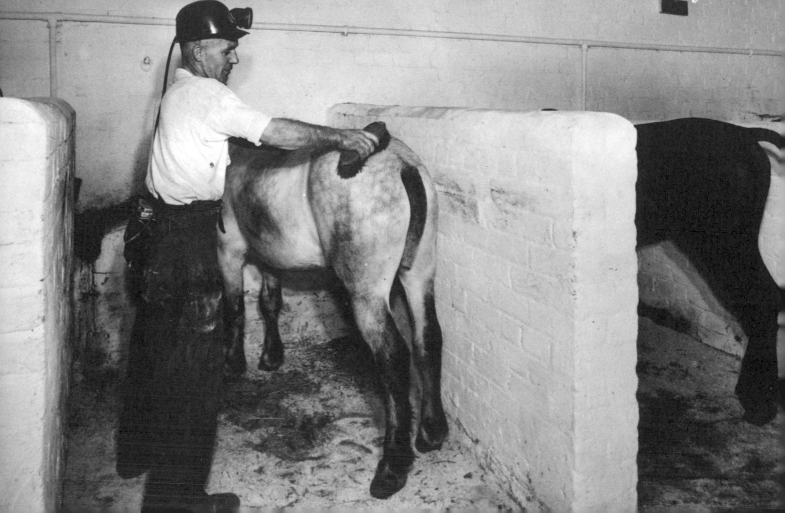

. . . the job they did was hauling tubs
of coal along the narrow gauge rail
tracks from the coal-face to the foot
of the pit-head shaft.

It was a job that could best be done
by ponies, for in the smallest breeds,
like the Shetlands, there is great power
concentrated into small packages. In
fact, size for size, the Shetlands are
the strongest horse creature of all.

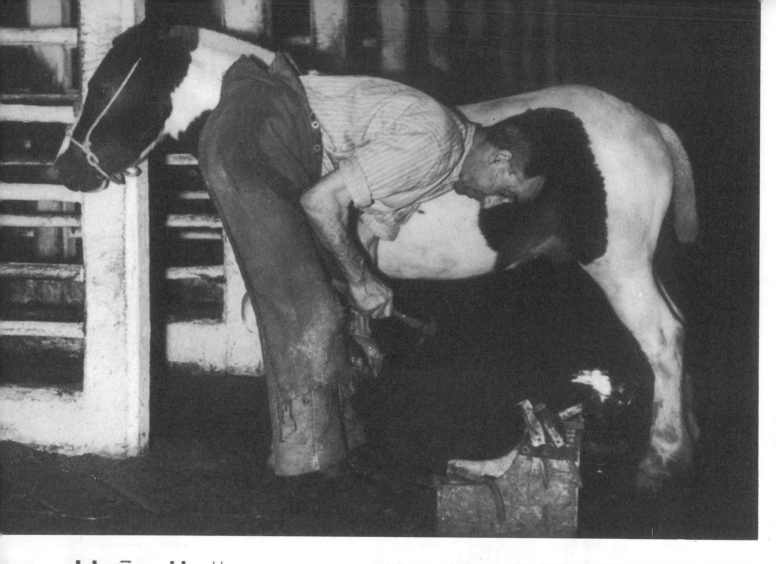

Ever seen a Shetland with a short coat? The long coat of the "Sheltie" was cropped short for mining, in the interests of cleanliness.

In the bad old days, pit ponies spent their entire lives below ground. They were stabled and fed in the deep darkness of the mine, and they never saw a green field, or the blue of the sky.

But gradually the ponies were replaced by machinery, and now there are hardly any ponies left working below ground in the coal mines. Those that still labour alongside the miners are well treated, and have their regular "holidays" above ground.

A PONY OF YOUR VERY OWN

When you have a pony of your very own,
something very special happens to you,
if you are a pony person . . .
Suddenly you have got four extra legs,
two more eyes, and a new set of perceptions,
for riding your own pony is not at all
like riding a pony that anyone rides.
And it works the other way, too, for
you have a lot to give your pony . . .
It is in the scheme of creation that
ponies (and horses) only become the
most and the best that they can become
in partnership with a human being.

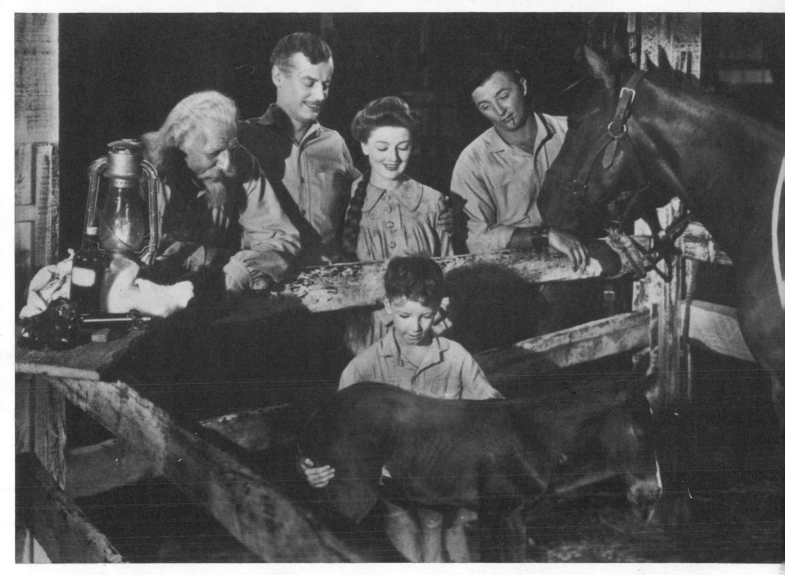

John Steinbeck wrote a book about a boy and a pony, called The Red Pony. It is a great book, and one you should read. Here is a tiny taste of its flavour. . . .

A RED pony colt was looking at him out of the stall, Its tense ears were forward and a light of disobedience was in its eyes. Its coat was rough and thick as an airedale's fur and its mane was long and tangled. Jody's throat collapsed in on itself and cut his breath short.

"He needs a good currying," his father said, and if I ever hear of you not feeding him or leaving his stall dirty, I'll sell him off in a minute."

Jody couldn't bear to look at the pony's eyes any more. He gazed down at his hands for a moment, and he asked very shyly, "Mine?" No one answered him. He put his hand out towards the pony. Its grey nose came close, sniffing loudly, and then the lips drew back and the strong teeth closed on Jody's fingers. The pony shook its head up and down and seemed to laugh with amusement. Jody regarded his bruised fingers. "Well," he said with pride—"well, I guess he can bite all right." The two men laughed, somewhat in relief. Carl Tiflin went out of the barn and walked up a side-hill to be by himself, for he was embarrassed, but Billy Buck stayed. It was easier to talk to Billy Buck. Jody asked him again—"Mine?"

DAY'S END...

Here's memories, they're all he has,
now sight and strength are fled;
He's run his race, he's done his work,
all that's to say's been said.
Memories. Was his that world,
so huge, green, strange and new
That he, a foal on stilty legs,
chasing his mother, knew?
A foal? Him? Old, feeble, slow,
finding scant taste in new green grass,
Each step a toil, each sight so dim,
When once he'd race a moth to pass?
It all flits by him, as he sits,
warm in the morning sun,
It doesn't fret his placid mind,
that all is past and done,
His memories are warm and good,
seen through his life's long view,
For now, at his sunset, they alone,
are all that's really true. . . .

There are people we must thank, now that we have come to the end of our book, and first, we are very grateful to Mrs. Breach, of Firs Farm, for letting us photograph her splendid Palomino pony, who appears on our front cover. Then there were the folk at Brookshill farm, on Harrow Weald, who made us welcome to picture their many fine ponies. And the International League for the Protection of Horses gave our photographer every help at Cherry Tree farm, their Home of Rest in Surrey. The Pit Pony pictures came from the files of the Coal Board, and the Horse Bus from the archives of London Transport. The Press Office of the American Embassy provided our "Western" pictures, and the Irish Tourist Board the splendid Pony Trekking set, and the colour spread of "Stable Yard". Our Milk pony came from Unigate. Photographer Jane Bown provided many lovely pictures, such as the one facing this page. Many more fine pictures came from Fox photos, and the Sport and General Agency. "World of Horses" came from the book of that name by James Reynolds, by courtesy of the publishers, Hutchinson's. The extract from John Steinbeck's "Red Pony" was printed here by permission of the publishers William Heinemann, Ltd., and "A Few Words from a Horse" came from "Thoughts on Riding", by Brigadier Lyndon Bolton, by courtesy of Messrs Matthew Hodder. "Red Indian Horse Talk" came from "The Horse in Blackfoot Indian Culture" by John Ewers, published by the Smithsonian Institution.

Finally our thanks are due to Miss Turnbull's pony David, for carrying our photographer round so patiently. He lives at the stables of St. Theresa's convent, Effingham, Surrey.